My First Book of
MARCHES

25 Favorite Pieces
in Easy Piano Arrangements

Dolly M. Moon

Illustrated by
Karen E. Goldsmith

DOVER PUBLICATIONS, INC., NEW YORK

Dedicated to the memory of Diane

Published in Canada by General Publishing Company, Ltd., 30 Lesmill Road, Don Mills, Toronto, Ontario.

Published in the United Kingdom by Constable and Company, Ltd., 3 The Lanchesters, 162–164 Fulham Palace Road, London W6 9ER.

My First Book of Marches: 25 Favorite Pieces in Easy Piano Arrangements is a new work, first published by Dover Publications, Inc., in 1990.

Manufactured in the United States of America
Dover Publications, Inc., 31 East 2nd Street, Mineola, N.Y. 11501

Library of Congress Cataloging-in-Publication Data

My first book of marches.

Summary: Includes Dixie, Semper fidelis, American patrol, and When the saints go marching in.
1. Marches (Piano), Arranged—Juvenile. [1. Marches (Piano), Arranged. 2. Piano music] I. Moon, Dolly M. II. Goldsmith, Karen E., ill.
M1378.M9855 1990   90-751607
ISBN 0-486-26338-X (pbk.)

Contents

Introduction

Most marches were composed for military bands to play for marching troops. But almost any kind of music may become a march, and marches may be played for a variety of occasions. Marches may start out as popular songs, even love songs. They may be folk music or classical music. They may be bouncy and humorous. They may be slow and sad. They may be used for weddings or for funerals.

The 25 marches in this book include all of these types. Many of them came from England, France, Germany, and other countries, but they all took root in America and have become part of our musical tradition.

The Liberty Bell: John Philip Sousa, known as "The March King," wrote this march in 1893 soon after forming his famous band. The march honors a well-known symbol of American independence, which first rang to celebrate the reading of the Declaration of Independence in Philadelphia in 1776.

When the Saints Go Marching In: This hymn, probably written by James Black around 1896, became the most famous of Dixieland jazz tunes. It has been one of the tunes played to accompany funeral processions in New Orleans, which sometimes became very fast and cheerful shortly after they had left the graveyard.

The Battle Hymn of the Republic: This was the great anthem of the Union soldiers in the Civil War. The tune was first used for a revival hymn. In 1861, the year when the war began, Julia Ward Howe wrote her lyrics beginning "Mine eyes have seen the glory" after hearing troops singing this tune with other words.

El Capitan: Sousa composed many operettas (light operas), one of which was called *El Capitan* ("The Captain" in Spanish). This march from 1896 combined two songs from the operetta.

Hail to the Chief: For over 150 years, Americans have played this piece when the President makes an official appearance. But it was originally a song glorifying a Scottish Highlands chieftain, with words by the English poet and novelist Walter Scott.

Bridal March: Most Americans know this tune as "Here Comes the Bride," and it is traditionally played when the bride walks down the aisle toward the altar. In Wagner's opera *Lohengrin* (first performed in 1850), this music is sung while the hero and his bride are being escorted to their home after the wedding.

The Yellow Rose of Texas: This song was written in 1858 by an unknown songwriter for use in the popular minstrel shows. When the Civil War broke out three years later, it became a favorite of both sides in the conflict. It is now the state song of Texas.

Tramp! Tramp! Tramp! the Boys Are Marching: The Civil War produced such fine songs as *When Johnny Comes Marching Home, Marching Through Georgia,* and *Tenting on the Old Camp Ground.* Two of the Civil War marches by George F. Root have never lost their popularity: *The Battle Cry of Freedom* and this march from 1863.

March of the Three Kings: This rousing Christmas carol describes the procession of the three kings to Bethlehem. It has been sung in southern France for seven hundred years.

Columbia, the Gem of the Ocean: This patriotic march has been sung and played in America since the 1840s.

Yankee Doodle: This nonsense song was probably written in the early 1770s. Several years later, it became the most popular song of the Revolutionary War, sung by both Americans and British soldiers. The word "Yankee" was being used much earlier, but no one really knows what the word (or the song) was originally supposed to mean.

Dixie: The minstrel shows were at their peak in 1859 when Dan Emmett took off two hours to write this wonderful song for his minstrel troupe. Everyone loved it from the start. Emmett was a Northerner, and *Dixie* (which he called a "Plantation Song and Dance") wasn't meant to be taken seriously in any way, but the Confederate troops took it up as a march and it became the unofficial anthem of the Confederacy in the Civil War.

Semper Fidelis: Sousa was conductor of the U.S. Marine Band when he wrote this march in 1888. He dedicated it to the Marine Corps, and it became their official march. "Semper fidelis" (which means "Always faithful" in Latin) is their motto.

Funeral March: Chopin wrote this sorrowful piece in 1837 and later included it in one of his piano sonatas. It has sometimes been used at state funerals.

Entry of the Gladiators: This light-hearted march was written by a Czech bandmaster in 1900. It soon came to be used for the "Entry of the Clowns" at the circus and the "Entry of the Wrestlers" at showy wrestling matches.

Wedding March: The wedding of the Duke of Athens in Shakespeare's play *A Midsummer Night's Dream* was the occasion for this joyful march, written by Mendelssohn in 1842. It became so beloved that it is now the music usually played when the bride and groom walk down the aisle at the end of the wedding ceremony.

Funeral March of a Marionette: In cartoons and at Halloween shows, you will hear this eerie piece. It perfectly mimics the bouncy, abrupt movements of a marionette (a puppet hung from strings). Charles Gounod wrote the march in 1872.

Washington Post March: The *Washington Post* is one of the oldest and best-known newspapers in America. In 1889, Sousa (who then lived in Washington) honored it with this march.

Turkish March: As you have seen, marches were often used in operas and plays. In 1811 Beethoven wrote music for the play *The Ruins of Athens,* including this march for the conquering Turkish army. While playing it, try to imitate the kettledrums, cymbals, and jingling bells that the Turkish band would have been playing.

The Stars and Stripes Forever!: This is the most famous march that Sousa ever wrote. He composed it on a ship returning to the United States in 1896.

Toreador March: This fine march comes from the 1875 opera *Carmen* by the French composer Georges Bizet. The crowds sing it for the procession of the bullfighter Escamillo to the bullring with his Gypsy sweetheart Carmen.

Marche Militaire: The great Franz Schubert wrote about twenty marches. This is the best known of them all, written in 1826.

American Patrol: This march was written by Frank W. Meacham in 1885. During the Second World War it was sung to the words "We must be vigilant."

The Marines' Hymn: The French composer Jacques Offenbach originally wrote this melody as a song for two soldiers in one of his operettas in 1867. It got its new words ("From the halls of Montezuma") around 1918 and became the theme of the U.S. Marines.

The Yankee Doodle Boy: Most people call this song "Yankee Doodle Dandy." George M. Cohan wrote it for a musical in 1904 and gave it patriotic words almost as nonsensical as those for *Yankee Doodle.* (Can you hear where it borrows the music of *Yankee Doodle*?) The tune is so catchy that it sends marchers swinging down the street.

The Liberty Bell

John Philip Sousa

1

When the Saints Go Marching In

James M. Black

A

D   D7   G

Gm   D   A   D

The Battle Hymn of the Republic

American traditional

El Capitan

John Philip Sousa

Hail to the Chief

James Sanderson

Bridal March

(from *Lohengrin*)

Richard Wagner

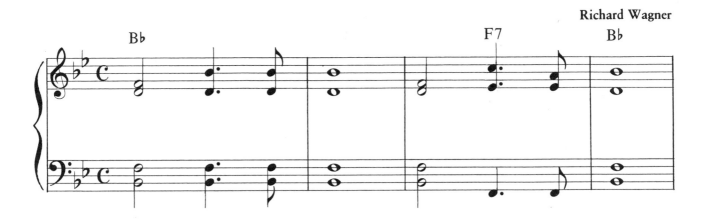

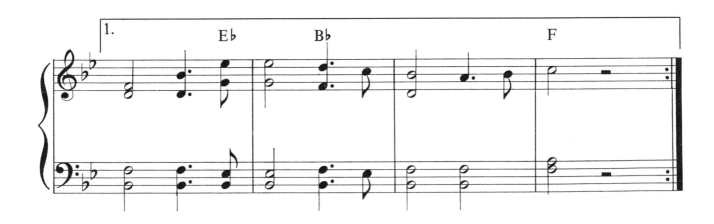

The Yellow Rose of Texas
(secondo)

American traditional

Introduction

The Yellow Rose of Texas

(primo)

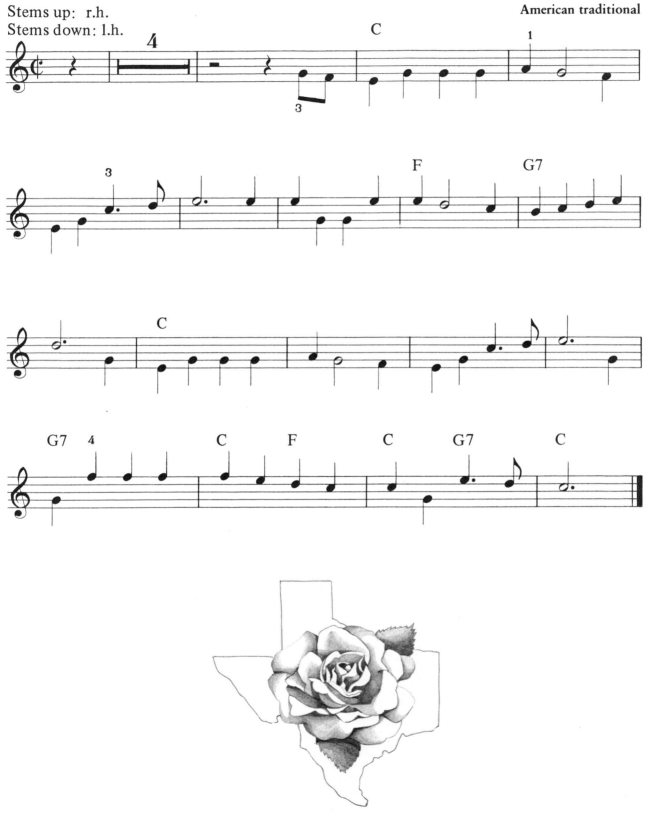

Stems up: r.h.
Stems down: l.h.

American traditional

11

Tramp! Tramp! Tramp!
the Boys Are Marching

George F. Root

Refrain

March of the Three Kings

French traditional

Columbia, the Gem of the Ocean

Thomas à Beckett

Yankee Doodle

American traditional

Dixie

(secondo)

Daniel D. Emmett

Refrain

20

Dixie
(primo)

Stems up: r.h.
Stems down: l.h.

Daniel D. Emmett

Semper Fidelis

John Philip Sousa

Funeral March

Frédéric Chopin

23

Entry of the Gladiators

(R.H. *8ᵛᵃ segue* on repeat)

Julius Fučík

Wedding March

(from *A Midsummer Night's Dream*)

Felix Mendelssohn

Funeral March of a Marionette

Charles Gounod

Washington Post March

John Philip Sousa

Turkish March

(from *The Ruins of Athens*)

Ludwig van Beethoven

The Stars and Stripes Forever!

John Philip Sousa

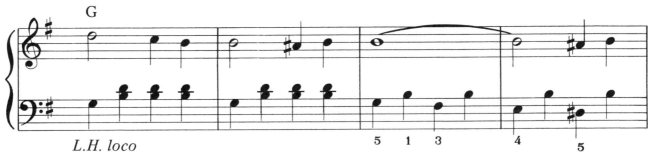

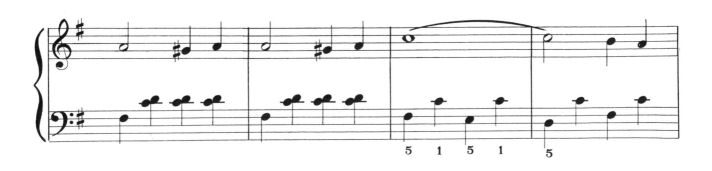

Toreador March

(from *Carmen*)

Georges Bizet

Marche Militaire

Franz Schubert

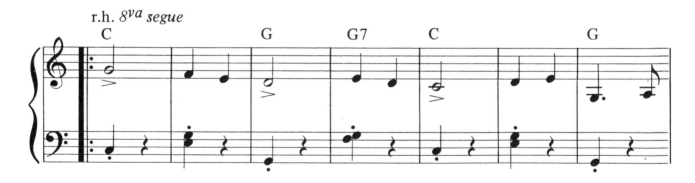

American Patrol

Frank W. Meacham

The Marines' Hymn

Jacques Offenbach

The Yankee Doodle Boy

George M. Cohan

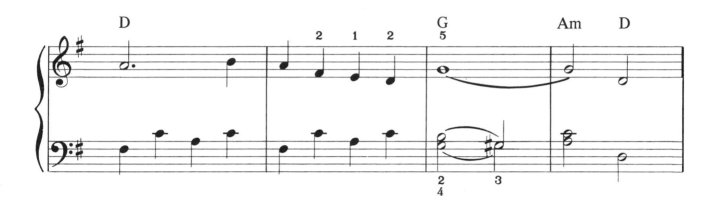

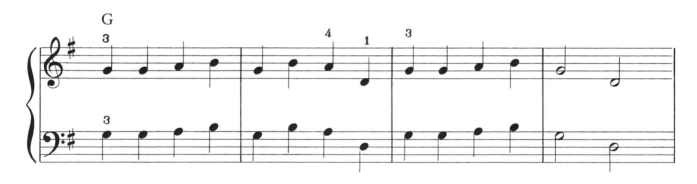

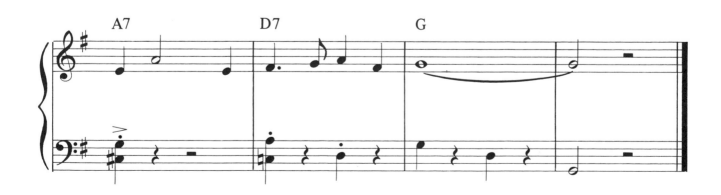